The Waterman/Harewood Piano Series

JOSEF GRUBER

Two at the Piano

50 duets for Young Pianists

edited by

Fanny Waterman

and

Marion Harewood

Faber Music Limited

London

Two AT THE PIANO contains 50 duets for the young pianist to play with a teacher or more advanced player. They are carefully graded, progressing from simple five-finger patterns, with the hands in octaves, to independent parts for each hand.

Playing duets can, and should be, an exciting adventure, like rowing a boat together or riding a bicycle made for two. Not only is it fun in itself, but it naturally leads the young pianist to listen very carefully to the other part and thus to develop ensemble playing. For duets involve learning to start (and end!) together and to match as closely as possible rhythm, dynamics, mood and tone colour. When all this is successfully achieved, *Two at the Piano* will feel, and sound, like *One at the Piano*.

F.W. and M.H.

Czech edition *ABC* first published in 1967
© 1967 by Editio Supraphon, Prague
This edition first published in 1979 by Faber Music Ltd
3 Queen Square, London WC1N 3AU
by arrangement with Editio Supraphon
English text and music editing © 1979 by Faber Music Ltd
Cover design by Shirley Tucker
Printed in England by Caligraving Ltd
All rights reserved

Contents

1	Two at the Piano	5
2	Climbing up	5
3	Come and Play with Me	5
4	Mother's Day	7
5	Sunshine	7
6	Little John	9
7	If I were a Shepherd	9
8	A Sad Memory	11
9	Country Revels	13
10	Never Give Up	13
11	Folksong	13
12	In the Sulks	13
13	Springtime	15
14	In a Happy Mood	15
15	The Showman	17
16	In the Garden	19
17	Waltz	19
18	Greetings	21
19	Happy and Sad	23
20	Carefree	23
21	The Lively Rascal	25
22	O to be Home Again	25
23	Gossip	27
24	At the Blacksmith	27
25	With Abandon	29
26	Speech is Silver – Silence is Golden	29
27	Waltz	31
28	The Skylark	31
29	The Little Horseman	33
30	A Song is Good Company	33
31	Andante from Haydn's Symphony No. 94	35
32	Thoughts from the Past	35
33	By the Stream	37
34	In a Gondola	39
35	The Two Folksingers	39
36	Full of Fun	41
37	To my Brother	41
38	A Short Story	43
39	Evening Song	43
40	High Spirits	45
41	In Joy and In Sorrow	45
42	Saying Goodbye	47
43	Mazurka	47
44	Let's Have a Party	49
45	Coming Home	49
46	Flirting	51
47	The Huntsmen	51
48	The Little Drummer	53
49	Bubbling Over	55
50	Song of the Mermaid from Weber's *Oberon*	55

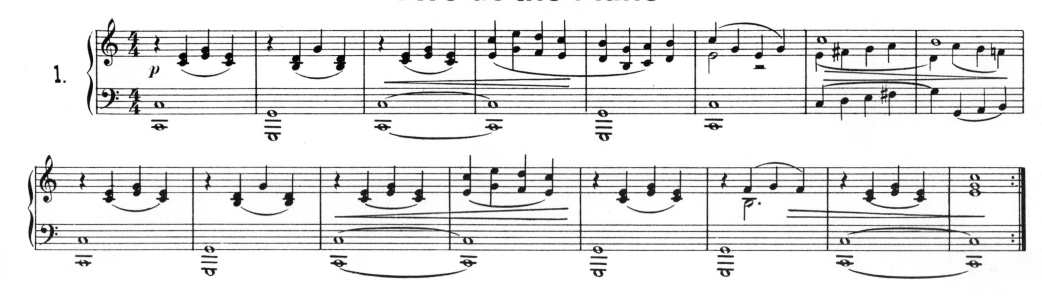

Two at the Piano

1.

Climbing up

2.

Come and Play with Me

3.

Two at the Piano

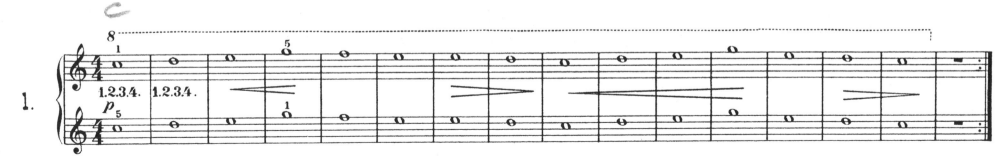

Climbing up

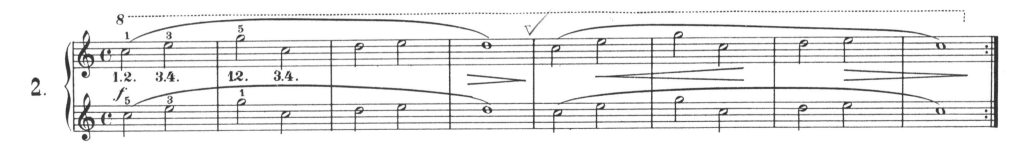

Come and Play with Me

Mother's Day

Sunshine

Mother's Day

Sunshine

Little John

If I were a Shepherd

Little John

If I were a Shepherd

A Sad Memory

Country Revels

A Sad Memory

Country Revels

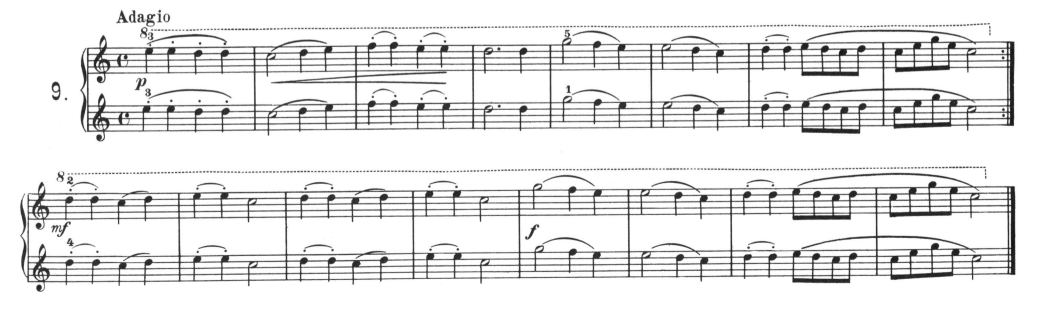

Never Give Up

Folksong

In the Sulks

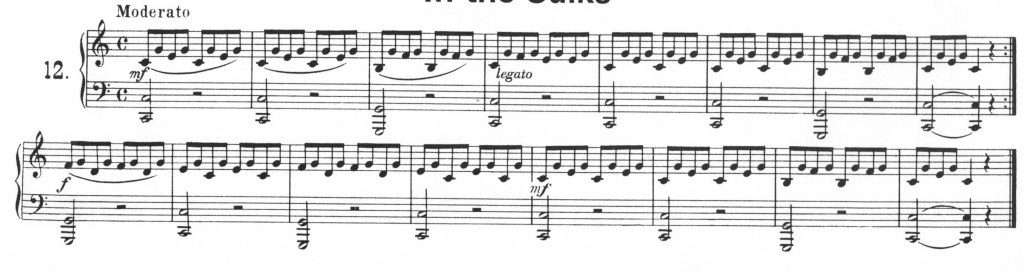

Never Give Up

10.

Folksong

11.
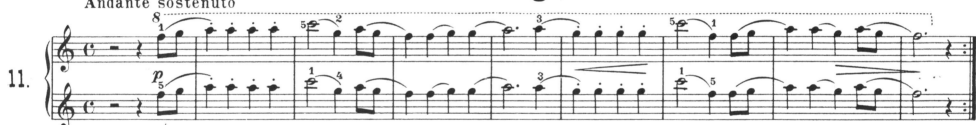

In the Sulks

12.

Springtime

In a Happy Mood

Springtime

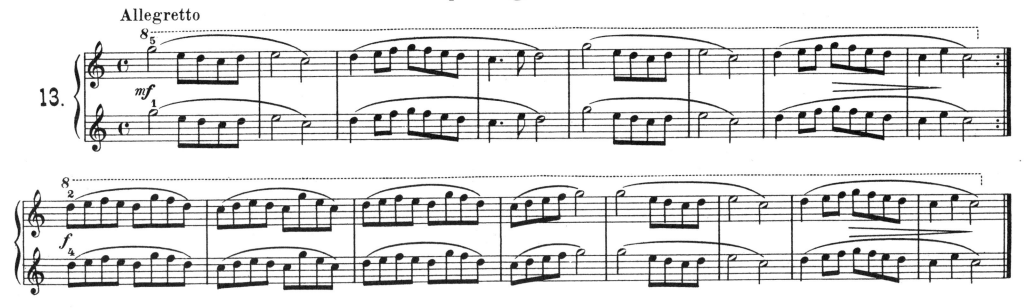

In a Happy Mood

The Showman

The Showman

Andante con moto

15.

In the Garden

Waltz

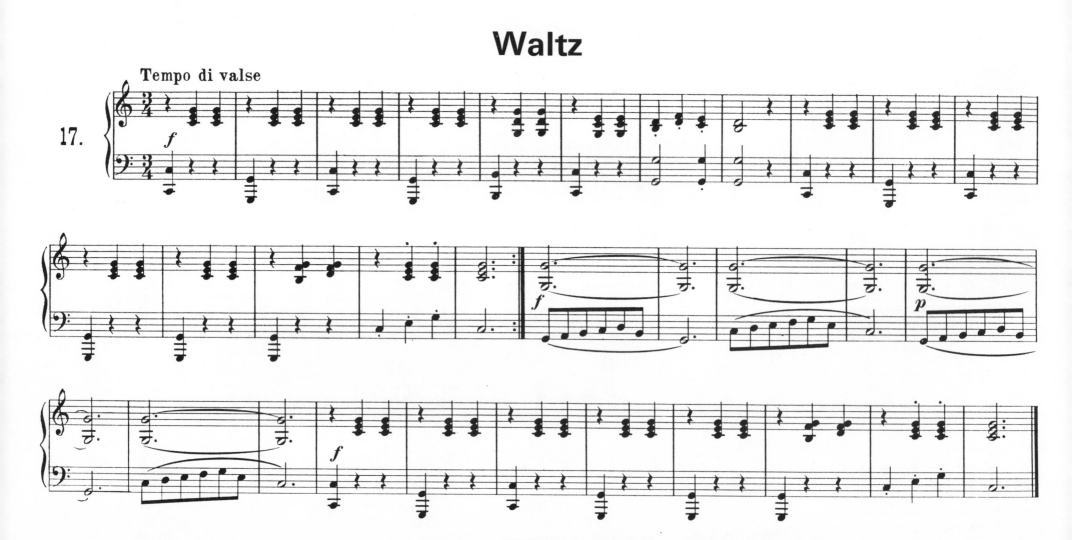

In the Garden

Waltz

Greetings

Greetings

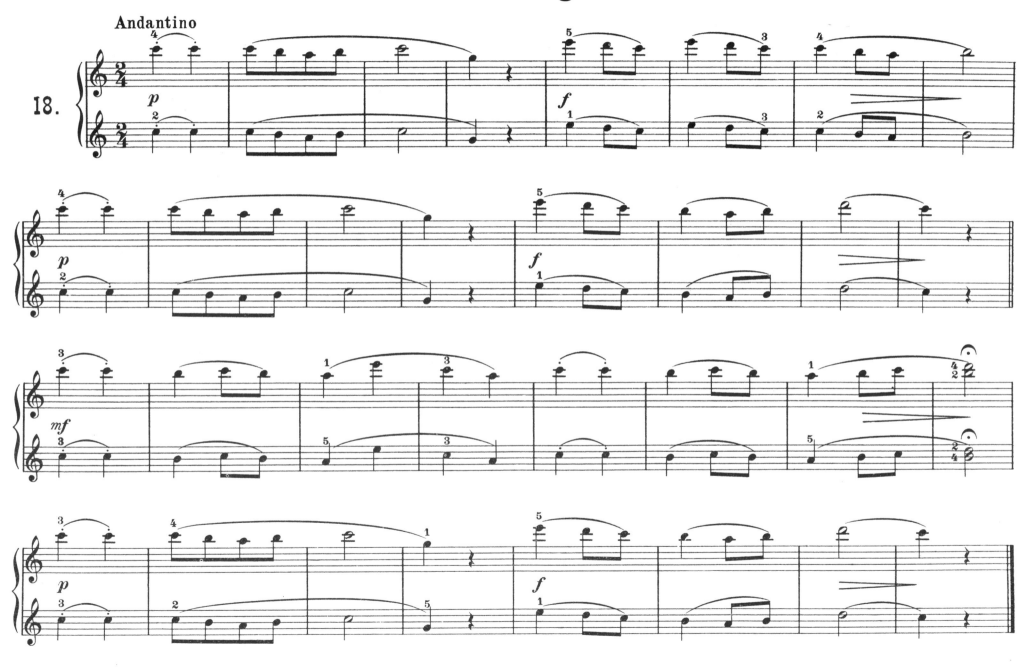

Happy and Sad

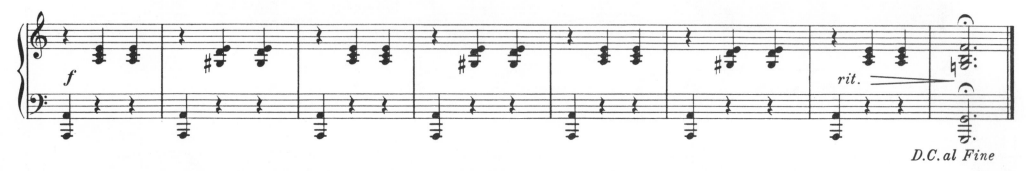

Carefree

Happy and Sad

Carefree

The Lively Rascal

O to be Home Again

The Lively Rascal

O to be Home Again

Gossip

At the Blacksmith

In this piece the second player's right arm is positioned below the first player's left arm

Gossip

At the Blacksmith

With Abandon

Speech is Silver—Silence is Golden

D.C. al Fine

With Abandon

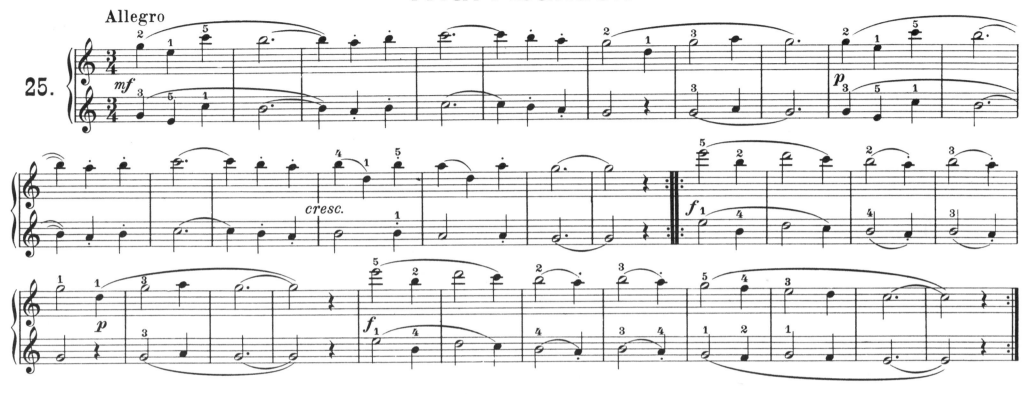

Speech is Silver—Silence is Golden

Waltz

The Skylark

Waltz

The Skylark

The Little Horseman

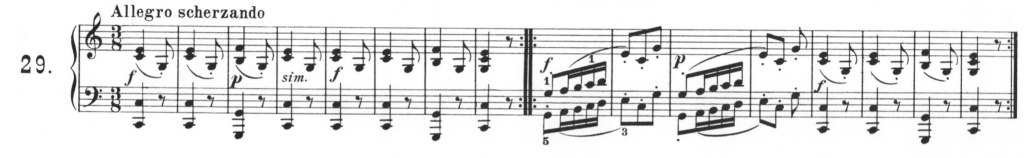

A Song is Good Company

The Little Horseman

A Song is Good Company

Andante from Haydn's Symphony No.94

Thoughts from the Past

Andante from Haydn's Symphony No.94

31.

Thoughts from the Past

Adagio ma non troppo

32.

By the Stream

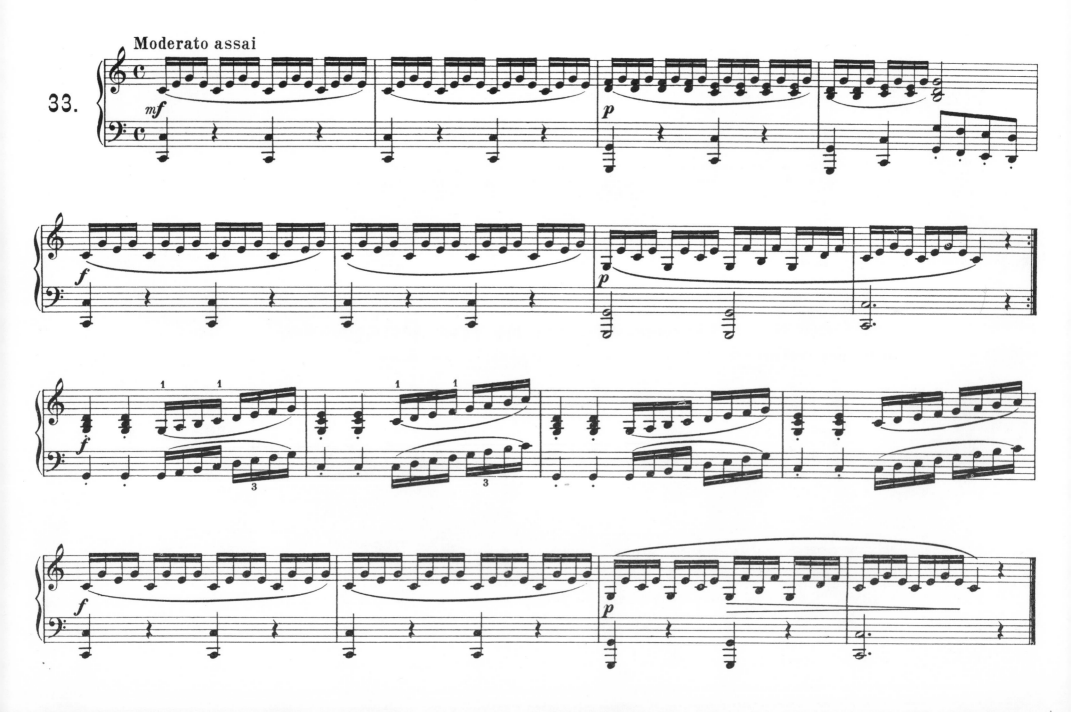

By the Stream

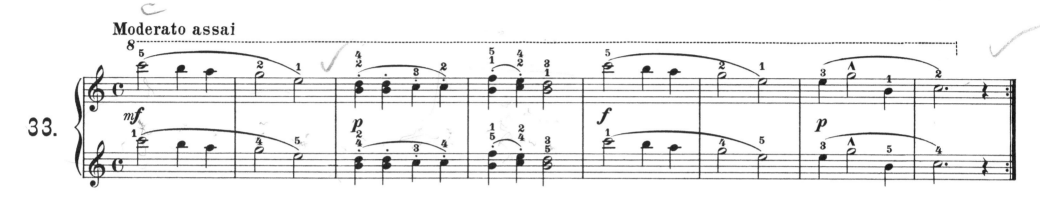

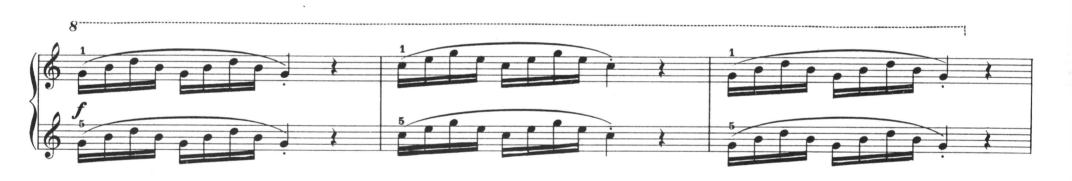

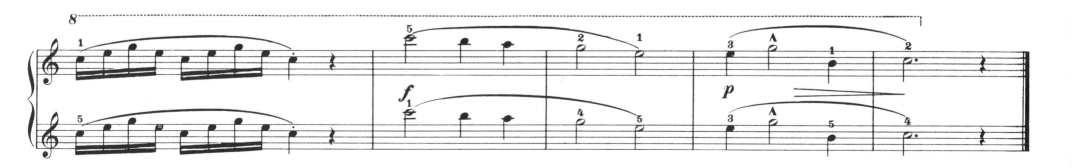

In a Gondola

The Two Folksingers

In a Gondola

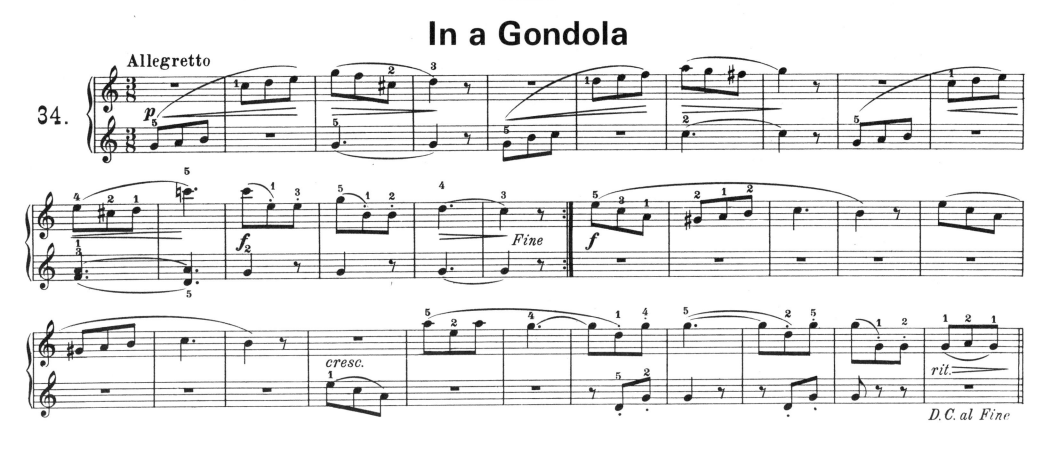

The Two Folksingers

Full of Fun

To my Brother

Full of Fun

To my Brother

A Short Story

Evening Song

D.C. al Fine

A Short Story

Evening Song

D. C. al Fine

High Spirits

In Joy and In Sorrow

High Spirits

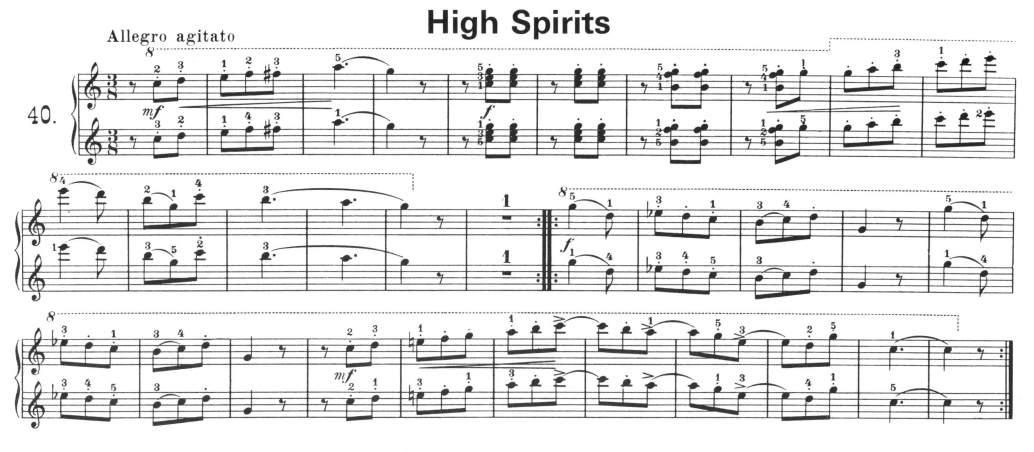

In Joy and In Sorrow

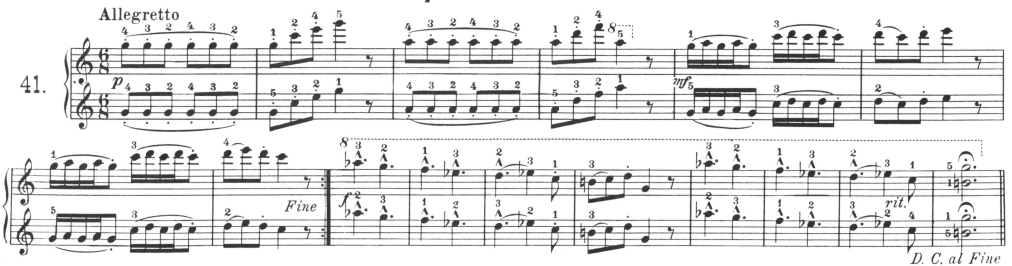

D. C. al Fine

Saying Goodbye

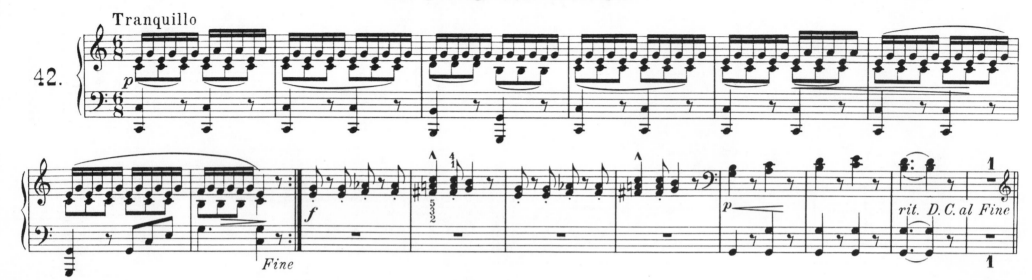

Mazurka

Saying Goodbye

Mazurka

Let's Have a Party

Coming Home

Let's Have a Party

Coming Home

Flirting

The Huntsmen

Flirting

The Huntsmen

The Little Drummer

The Little Drummer

Bubbling Over

Song of the Mermaid from Weber's *Oberon*

Bubbling Over

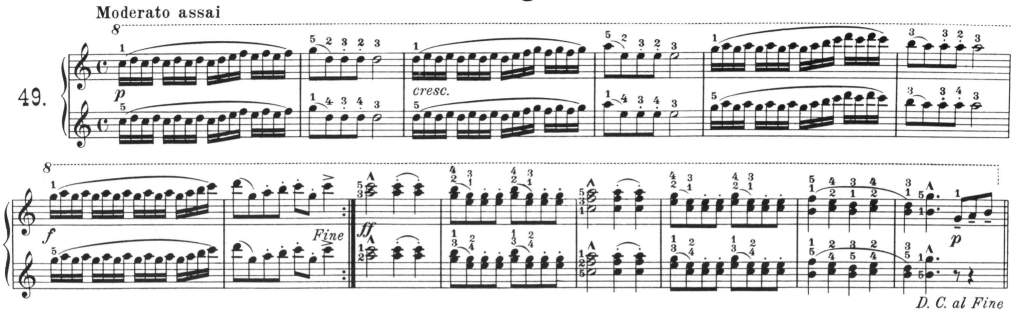

Song of the Mermaid from Weber's *Oberon*